sweet mellow red

Hometown Proud!

Dic
Hml

sweet mellow red

love like wine

WILLIAM R. HUDSON

Excerpts from "Wisdom From the Celtic World" © 2005
John O'Donohue used with permission from the publisher,
Sounds True, Inc.

Library of Congress Cataloging-in-Publication Data
Hudson, William R., 1981—
Sweet Mellow Red : Love Like Wine / William R. Hudson
p. cm.
ISBN: 978-1-7350322-0-7 (paperback)
LCCN: 20200914004
1. Spiritual life   2. Friendship—Religious aspects—Christianity
3. Wine   4. Hudson, William R.—Biography   I. Title

Book Design by: David Provolo
Cover Design by: David Provolo
Cover Art by: William C. Tippie
Author Photograph by: Charity Hedges

horiZen Publishing LLC
Versailles, KY 40383
horizenpublishing@gmail.com
10 9 8 7 6 5 4 3 2 1

dedication

Rooted in Memory

Mountains, rivers, and trees. Individual elements of Earth that each have roots, yet whose systems intertwine: Ancient snow-capped stone with foundations that reach warmth below, under-ground tributaries whose waters gather in the dark and emerge into the light; kind waters offering a drink to all who thirst, and leaves green with life rustling in the wind whilst wooden fingers travel deep the mire—around stone, in search of water—to anchor the existence of growth above.

I suppose the human person is most like a tree—we have life and experience growth, but we have nothing, no physical exten-sion, to hold us firm in place. Our blood and ancestry can sometimes lead us to places where we discover belonging; memory, however, is our truest anchor and will hold us near our Source.

There is a mountain beneath our souls and within the blood of our veins, a river of life. What shall our hands create and bring forth into the light? Our memories are collections of what we will become. What we choose to remember gathers in the dark and what we imagine will pool into the light. The cup we offer to those who thirst will become the purest existence we have here; kind water for parched lips...eternal love that washes over the soul.

Each loving act a new memory; roots that hold us firm.

—For Katherine

contents

prologue

It was on the treadmill at work that I first began to develop a relationship with the birch trees outside the window. Or, maybe, I began to realize a relation that had always been there. On the second floor of a high-rise building in downtown Louisville, Kentucky, I often imagined that I was running briskly along the rocky shore of the Mediterranean Sea. This was well before treadmills allowed you to select a run through: Wild California, downtown Chicago, the countryside of Italy, or the Trinity Mountains.

I have yet to select one of these programmed experiences. I prefer instead to stare out the long row of windows, through the wispy leaves of four beautiful birch trees, watching as the rising sun sends rays of light between their branches. In the soft morning light, I feel somehow *changed*. As I run and breathe, I wonder how flat images on a treadmill screen could ever awaken my soul to the serenity of the "Trinity Mountains" or how electronic images could ever reach me more deeply than the calming presence of birch trees swaying just outside the window. I am still learning to recognize and appreciate the Beauty that I encounter on a daily basis. Sometimes there are glimpses of this in nature; other times we happen along another person as an oasis, affording a drink to our soul.

What is true now, was true then. When a person's soul truly awakens is when the discoveries of our essential connections to nature and to others becomes most apparent.

Pondering these connections, I run on a loop like a hamster on a wheel—a cog in the middle of Corporate America, with the birch trees here to console me. Not to say that I have viewed my corporate setting as a cage; like any young person—back then, fresh out of college—I was ready to play my part of change in the world.

That was years ago, and upon accepting a position with the company, I embarked on a large-scale project to help build a software system meant for managing the operations of three separate companies, a complex system that would help the companies function more as one.

Large-scale projects like this utilize the skill sets of various groups of people to accomplish daunting objectives. Such endeavors continue to extend us very limited budgets—and consequently pressing deadlines. Tensions run high when projects are over budget or when tasks are running behind schedule.

Often, a pair of firm hands on your shoulders can help ease the stress when deadlines are near—until you consider, *Whose are the hands rubbing my shoulders?*

The hands belonged to Kathy, an "older" lady.

And that being the first time that Kathy had reached out

to massage my neck, I found myself thinking, *Does she just want to touch a pair of young shoulders, or does she sense my tension and genuinely want to ease my spirits?* Regardless, my tight shoulders gave way as my breathing slowed and my worries began to melt away.

It was not until weeks later—as both her hands cradled my face—that I found in her eyes and felt in her touch the gentleness of a grandmother, the loving affection of a mother, and the kindred spirit of a true friend. Although Kathy was neither of the former, she has definitely proven to be the latter, and through her eyes I remember seeing glimpses that assured me she possessed the qualities of all three.

Our meeting was over ten years ago, in a time I would never have needed to consider *how might a writer frame this approach?*

As an invitation into Kathy's story, how about you imagine that you are having your shoulders rubbed. Your mind is slipping away, and you find yourself running through a grove of olive trees, their gnarled roots winding down under foot....

Or—perhaps closer to home—you are on a footpath in the hills of Kentucky, racing beside a simmering stream. The stream turns down by the old milk house where the cool of the water keeps the milk at a temperature ideal for storage. Let your thoughts take you back to a time when folks churned their own butter; those are the hands who still know the secrets of how to turn milk into cheese! And let me finally lead you by the hand up over the hill into a field of grain, golden husks blowing rhythmically in the wind.

Now into the small house. A dark, wooden table is set with olives and cheese, and the warmth of the room is laced with the aroma of rosemary and thyme. A loaf of freshly baked bread sits at the table's edge. But something is missing from the table's top: a sweet, bottled presence that later will join all those that sit round the hearth, a spirit that offers belonging... something mellow and red.

love like wine

True love is like a fine wine: sweet and mellow and red.

I believe there is a reason that certain people enter our lives. Some individuals are sent to remind us of the hardness of the human heart...they are barren grounds where little can grow. Others have souls of rich soil that give nourishment to green vines and sweet fruits. There are very few hearts, however, that yield a grape so exquisite that you yearn to bottle it up. Oh, to know such a person whose presence could be uncorked in a time of great despair; to know a love that can be trusted to pour its light into unknown, unsheltered nights.

I have the pleasure of knowing a person like this, a lady with red hair that shines auburn in the sunlight and whose blue eyes, at times, are as green as the sea shallows following a storm. Eyes that are wreathed in a deep, misty blue that always betrays the depth that lies beneath. She has a presence that pours over you as peace...and grace...and love. I have often pondered the mystery of what forms a person with a nature such as this. This person who has become the truest of friends to me.

Katherine—a lady that I call Sweet Mellow Red.

Great wines may indeed be dependent on rich soils, exposure to the sun, and high elevations. But there are other influences that make a great wine: tradition, for instance, and the careful attention of he whose hands work the vineyard. The creation of a "great vintage" is, in and of itself, an act of the truest love.

I will admit that I know very little of the production of wine, and less of fine wines—little of the art and great care that go into making a wine 'fine'. Most of what I do know about wine is a collage of knowledge framed in picturesque vistas of false memory. Artificial moments collected through movie reels—powerfully artistic films—with backdrops of golden vineyards in the foothills of mountainous regions. Such scenes offer exhibitions of heartfelt moments, passionate romance, robust laughter, and deep love. It is love that stitches these tales together. Dramas, telling a story of fruits cultivated not just in geologic location but in the cradle of family tradition, rich culture, and a loving devotion to the vines. The wines in these stories are born works of art—beautiful portraits that influence all open to receiving their blessings. Katherine's story is a portrait such as this.

deep roots, rich soil

Roots that run deep reach a richness all their own.

"Where are you from?" Typically, the first question you ask after learning someone's name. Her name was Kathy, but her ID badge provided "KATHERINE." She had the reddest hair I had ever seen in my twenty-some years, and she stood about six feet tall with broad shoulders. Her eyes told me she had a kindred soul long before her actions ever would. Kathy was from Brodhead, Kentucky, from the head of the Dix River (in Rockcastle County). When she told me "Brodhead," I asked her to elaborate... "Where's that?" I asked. "Near Mount Vernon," she offered in the now familiar cadence of her low voice; a pleasant voice. I would soon learn that Brodhead was a one-horse town with only one caution light. Years after our meeting, as we continued in our many exchanges, she painted me quite a picture of her childhood. Her grandmother had been a school teacher in that area, and her mother was a teacher's aide. After school, she and her older (but shorter) sister, Kim, would sit at the local dairy freeze, Dairy Delight, and swing their feet under the red, patent leather bar stools. Elbows upon the counter, they would read Tiger Beat magazines or the Archie Comics while indulging in a tasty treat: Cherry Coke over crushed ice with a cheeseburger, or a dish of orange sherbet on other occasions.

Kathy's childhood home lay just seven miles down a no-name gravel road. She shared memories of skipping rope on the short gravel drive leading up to the house and said that if you walked up the drive you were likely to pass a couple bicycles turned over on their sides (streamers probably hanging from the handlebars...I did not ask). There was a small barn up to the left of the house, and in a cluster of trees tucked away, in the far distance on the right, there was an old, weather-worn school bus that served as a playhouse for the two girls. Their Papaw, Marshall, had been a school bus driver for years in the Ottawa area, and Kathy's Great Grandpaw John Oliver's wife Lizzy had founded the Ottawa Post Office and had actually named the area Ottawa. Lizzy being a relative of the legendary frontiersman Daniel Boone, it seemed fitting to me that Kathy's great grandmother would have named the territory her family had chosen to settle. And making Katherine's roots all the richer, one of her other great grandfathers, Webster, was kin to the famous country singer Loretta Lynn!

Sitting at my desk—in our office building downtown—I felt firm, but now familiar, hands on my shoulders. The red-haired woman sang us another folk classic (Loretta's "Coal Miner's Daughter") and eased the tension in my neck, yet again. Working on very complex and tedious tasks had stressed our team to the max in those days. Her songs and presence softened the mood of tense times for so many of us.

Right then, if Kathy had stopped and sung me a song from her childhood, I believe we would have become good friends more quickly than we did—that is, if Katherine had sung to me of being a dairy farmer's daughter instead of a coal miner's daughter. If she had sung to me of her roots that run so very deep, then I would have seen how she keeps a simple soul though we live in complicated, high-tech times; I would have begun to see where the richness of her young soul first sprouted its roots.

green, green vines

Our childhoods are green vines curling and climbing ever upward; budding fruits.

I imagine if Kathy had continued in her song, she would have invited us as guests into her memories, walking up the gravel drive and onto the narrow front porch of the old Thompson Place, the house she grew up in. A modest but homey place, it had shingled siding and four small, square posts propping up a roof overhead. From the front doorway she would show us into the living room where she and her sister often sat on the arms of their daddy's blue plaid chair, as he watched "My Three Sons" on a black and white television, his two beloved daughters close at his sides. A couple years before the eldest daughter came along, their mother, Charlotte, had given birth to a stillborn son, whose grave is marked Kevin Boone. Sadly, this would not be the only stillborn grave in the family plot. Kathy's older sister, Kim, would also lose her first child, another boy, Russell James, who years later would be laid to rest next to his uncle.

Six years after Kathy came along, though, she had a new baby brother, Gregory, who occupied a wooden crib in the center room of the house. On the opposite end of the center room was a coal stove heating the house, and from the kitchen, Kathy's momma would tell the girls when supper was ready. The kitchen was painted pale yellow with light wood cabinets. The girls would run into the kitchen, past an ironing board, and pull up to a white, metal, diner-style table with flecks of gold and silver sparkling in the finish. Shiny chrome legs curled from each corner, touching down to the worn linoleum floor at their feet, a sixties-green marble pattern with streaks of tan. After supper each night, Kathy would iron her daddy's uniform for the next day. Following service to his country in the 101st airborne, Billy Ray was a security officer at the Army Depot in Richmond by day, and he worked the family farm (three miles down the road) by night. The family had a couple hundred head of dairy cows, or at least they did until Billy's dad suffered a heart attack at age 65 and the extra work became too much to handle—so much work, in fact, that Billy would, some years later, have a heart episode of his own. Kathy's grandmother choosing to sell the cows would be the only viable alternative to challenging a man who would have worked himself into an early grave.

Little country girls want to know nothing of death, though; they just want to play house and run off in the woods, in an isolated world of imagination, to swing on great vines dangling down from the trees, swinging from this rock to that rock and having tea parties out on Big Flat Rock. The last verse of Kathy's song of memory would have shown us inside the old barn, dark timber walls adorned with magazine pictures of the celebrities Bobby Sherman and David Cassidy. These were treasured portraits of the girls' future husbands! Oh, the star-gazing eyes of our youth...such is the wonder that awakens in the minds of children! Why do we ever let that wonder get away from us, and how could we ever know what this harsh world holds for us?

the harsh elements

The green vines and budding fruits of our youth are eventually exposed to the harsh elements of this world.

Kathy once told me that she was indeed young and naïve when she left home. To quote her verbatim, she said, "Until I went to college I was deathly shy, highly naïve, and lived in a very protective environment. It didn't take much to embarrass me."

Didn't most of us feel "sheltered" before we entered the real world? Or perhaps was it the real, wider world that exposed our feelings of innocence and taught us where our vulnerabilities lay?

My friend has become a fine wine over time, but I suppose it was not until we sat back to back two days a week that our conversations began to deepen, and I began to realize the truth of her nature.

Now—no longer such a shy person—Kathy reminds me that it is still hard for her to know whom to trust with the hidden intimacies of her life. If the saying is true that "if you want to make an omelet, then you have to break some eggs," then it must be true that "if you want to make wine, then you have to crush some grapes."

Thus, until a grape is crushed under foot, the process of true growth has yet to be realized.

Really, it is a wonder to me that my friend has emerged so sweet and unspoiled when so many individuals caught in similar circumstances would have become unloving and bitter. She makes me believe that it is truly the struggles in our lives that strengthen us most and that only our trials can release from the depths *who* we really are.

Can we become better through each struggle? Yes—but *only* if we remain open and present through the passion as well as through the pain.

a fruit of passion

The sweetest fruit of the heart is passion, but with great passion comes the possibility of great pain.

I joke with Kathy about what I call the "Middle-Eastern Love Triangle" and how it is without a doubt my friend's red hair that has gotten her into trouble!

As the story goes, Kathy attended Eastern Kentucky University (EKU) in Richmond, where she eventually met two brothers from the Middle East—Amid and Aziz, from Qatar. Amid was attending EKU along with Kathy, while his brother Aziz (whom she would not meet until a few weeks later) was far to the south attending college in Florida. The two brothers, according to appearance, were "matched" to Kim and Kathy—in stature, anyway. Amid was the older, shorter of the two with darker skin, while Aziz had a far lighter complexion and a more commanding frame. Amid was attending EKU in training to become a military policeman, while Aziz often drove up from Florida, where he was studying to become an engineer.

One night, after working till a late hour in the arcade, Kathy locked up and decided to wind down in a 24-hour restaurant called "Peoples." It was here that she was first introduced to Amid, a young man that had a very flirtatious personality and showed unmistakable interest in Kathy.

Several days later, while Katherine walked home from class mid-afternoon, Amid pulled his vehicle to the roadside and offered her a ride home. After a shy refusal, Amid persisted and Kathy accepted. One of the first compliments Amid paid her in his flair of broken English was, "The first thing I think when I meet this women is: What beautiful hair!" Before Kathy walked into her house, Amid called back from her driveway and asked when he could "take her out." I suppose the flattery did the trick...some weeks later, Aziz was pleased to make the acquaintance of his brother's new girlfriend and tried to conceal that he was mad-struck with envy. Unknowingly, his eyes betrayed him, as Kathy had already detected a spark of interest beyond that which she had ever received from Amid. Sitting in the back seat of his brother's car, Aziz reached forward to the back of the passenger seat and began caressing Kathy's soft auburn hair; Amid did not take too kindly to this! "You keep your hands off my woman!" Amid commanded. And so, the lines of the triangle began to form.

Kathy stopped the story at this point and commented that both brothers had begun to refer to her as "Shweetie," an endearment, she felt, that was made more endearing by the pronunciation of their foreign tongue. She confessed to me that in the back of her mind, she knew Amid was committed to the military, that his time in America was limited, and that she had always seen a truer love in the eyes of the younger brother. This, however, did not change the fact that she still loved Amid and that his time in the States was drawing to a close.

In the months leading up to his departure, Amid focused his attention on preparing Kathy for his trip back home. Airport security, being lax as it was then, allowed Kathy and Aziz to accompany Amid to his gate, and they watched together as he walked steadily up the ramp to catch his plane. Through the tears in Katherine's eyes, a small figure turned to face them at the top of the ramp, hesitated, and then started back down toward them, shortening the distance. For all the steps that Amid had taken to ensure that Kathy would be ready for his departure, it was clear from his face that he had not properly prepared himself; tears welled and pooled in his eyes and then began streaming down his face as he walked back to meet them. What they both saw was the tender face of a man that rarely showed emotion. "Shweetie, take care about yourself. For Mr. Amid, he loves you."

The only word that Kathy could bring across her quivering lips was, "Goodbye."

This time, with no turn at the end of the ramp, Amid boarded the plane, leaving Katherine in the protective arms of his younger brother. As she watched the plane start toward the runway, it was the gentle hand of Aziz that led her away from the window, saying, "No, Shweetie. It is too much." I wonder if he saw in Katherine's eyes that she had truly, in that moment, said goodbye to his brother *for good*. Regardless, he wanted to spare her the heartache—spare her the wound—of watching the airliner disappear into the distance. How well Aziz had already come to know the fragility of my friend's heart.

I will give you fair warning, the next scene is straight out of a soap opera! As Amid was away in his home country of Qatar, Aziz made bi-weekly trips to Kentucky, driving those long hours to "check in on Kathy" and make sure that his "Shweetie" was doing alright. And so a greater bond began to grow between them through the thin facade of chivalry. Soon, Aziz asked Kathy to make a trip to the south, where the lines of familiar interaction became blurred, to say the least; this was when the true bloom of passion dawned its radiant face! Kathy had begun to fall deeply in love with the younger brother, and both were in agreement that they must spare Amid the hurt of announcing their newly-established relationship.

So after six months, when the older brother returned by plane for a short, final visit to the States, both brothers accompanied Katherine back to her home. And it was Amid who slept off his jet lag in her bedroom, while Aziz sat up on the couch, just on the other side of a thin wall, listening intently and trembling at the thought of the warm embrace that his elder brother was sharing on the other side.

Days later, Kathy assured Aziz that there were no details to be concerned of, but that night (being in the dark) was too much for Aziz to bear. He jumped into his Mustang and flung gravel from his tires as he peeled out of the drive! The next day—in a hushed exchange—he told Kathy he had gone to "see" his other girl, hoping that this false truth would build enough jealousy to tear the redhead from the clutches of his brother. Despite attempts at veiling the issue, Amid was acutely aware of what was going on. The night before his final departure (being put off by Kathy, yet again), Amid voiced his final words to Kathy: "My brother will never have you, for Mr. Amid will see to it!"

A Middle Eastern love triangle, indeed!

Just as there are various types of grapes, so there are various types of love. The flavors and characteristics of each are diverse. The love that grew between Aziz and Kathy after Amid's final return to Qatar was a love steeped in passion, but also a love that was proven true..."The truest love," she says, "I have ever known with another person."

Kathy once said to me, concerning this love, that "With much passion, comes the potential for much pain." The fruit of such a love is full and ripe—sweet to be sure—and the crushing of such a fruit is a bittersweet thing.

Katherine's heart was indeed broken three years later when Aziz was beckoned home. And when his cultural and family obligations mandated that he submit to an arranged marriage, a marriage to a bride of his mother's and father's choosing, it was a matter of respect that Aziz submit to his parents' wishes.

In the back of Kathy's mind, she had hoped and *believed* that Aziz would return to America and that, as an engineer, there would be plenty of employment opportunities for him in the States—surely he would not go through with this arranged marriage! The truth proved to be a truly crushing reality when Aziz never returned to her arms and instead took the hand of another.

safe in the bottle

Corked in a bottle, sealed off from the world, we think
we are safe and in control.

It takes time to heal from our wounds, and sometimes our deepest wounds never heal. We all need time, when such events transpire, to cordon ourselves off from the world, and in such times there are deep gestations and fermentations at work within. We become wines of signature notes, and our wounds remain as subtle hints of nutmeg, oak, and clove.

Thus it is with Katherine; but when she tells of the good times, I can almost always pick up on (in certain conversations) succulent undertones like blackberry currant and wild cherry—sweet memories which she chooses not to lose hold of, though they are laced with hurt.

It is indeed our experiences that form us into the people that we are all the while becoming, and it is only by the retelling of our experiences that we become known to others. Each experience ultimately becomes a fruit of a unique flavor, and we ourselves become a blend of passions and woes. The human person is ever-changing and continuously growing more mature with age. Following deep hurts, often we seek retreat in "safe" places and in relationships where we are less likely to be wounded; where we *think* we are safe from the world's harm. It is not "the world" that harms us, though, but rather individual people. And it is us, at times, that harm them…even if we are harming them with our innate tenderness and loyalty.

Enter Benny: a distinguished, older gentleman with salt and pepper hair, always well kept—never a hair out of place—and watery blue eyes. Kathy mentions that he was one handsome fella, looking kind of like Tom Brokaw. Kathy's mother once pointed out that "He is much better looking than Tom!" This was a safe move for Kathy, as Benny had been married a couple times and was almost the same age as Kathy's father—perfect for a young woman who was too wounded to have her heart captured again. And who has a more protective presence than a girl's father?

Six years Kathy had spent with Benny when finally, out of the blue, he announced that he was moving out. Benny moved himself into a small apartment.

Benny drove his milk truck (an eighteen wheeler) between Lexington and Louisville five days a week until one day, in the hot July heat, he blacked out at the wheel. So, one July day, Kathy unexpectedly got a call from a man she had not seen in six months, a man saying that the doctors had found a brain tumor, large in size and quite aggressive. Benny would not make it to the other side of that November.

On a Sunday, a few days before Thanksgiving, Benny called Kathy over to the house to explain why he had left her. Not because he did not love her, but because of how much he did. He was a man that never displayed emotion, now caught in a torrent of emotions. He told Kathy that he had left her because he knew she would never leave him and that because of his love for her, he had wanted her to find someone with whom she could spend her life.

My friend Katherine has a stone front and is a woman who only bears her emotions in private, so it was surprising (and a treasure to me) that when speaking of Benny, she allowed her emotion to be known. That conversation will forever be a defining moment to which I will cling, and it will always remind me of the depths that our friendship has reached. Each and every one of us needs friends such as this, friends that will help bear the weight of our own unique and personal human experience. We all need witnesses to our lives.

As strong and independent as Kathy had become, she would still tell you that feelings of a love realized are far easier to bear than being blindsided by a wave of emotional ferocity. Especially the billowing force of a love that has been shrouded from our view. Katherine's mother, Charlotte, called her on the phone to ask who would be attending Benny's visitation and funeral with her. Kathy answered that she did not *need* anyone to go with her. Such a blessing it was that her mother was at her side when Benny was placed into the back of the hearse, for the weakness in her knees became the proclamation of what they had shared, and what she feared she had lost.

Following the funeral, Benny's family discovered—between the pages of his Bible—many letters and cards written to him from Katherine. The photographs of Benny's daughter and of Katherine at a sick man's bedside were icons of love that remained for all to see and of love that still remained. Katherine, entering the bedroom of Benny's apartment, had this love reaffirmed as she collected her letters and whispered the word goodbye, again, into the absence of the room.

down into the cellar

Down into the cellar, hidden from sight, is a dark, red wine that yearns to meet the light.

To be aged properly it is best that wines are stored on their sides, at just the right temperature, and hidden away from sunlight. Our story takes us down into the cellar, where I am sure Kathy wishes certain details of these stories would remain.

But the contents of such experiences are far too valuable and much too rich to be left there in the dark forever.

The heart wants what the heart wants.[1] Enter Ray, a six-foot-four redhead with strong arms. With Ray, Kathy had met her true match, it seemed. More than once Kathy mentioned to me that there is nothing more attractive to her than a man tall enough and strong enough to effortlessly sweep her off her feet (as Ray did quite often). And Kathy, being broad-shouldered and of Scotch-Irish descent, stands about six feet tall herself, telling us just how strong her ideal man would have to be to stir the green in her eyes. This was another relationship of passion and of laughter. Benny's wish for Katherine had come partly true—she had met a younger man, though still five years her senior, and although she would spend thirteen years of her life with this man, she would not spend the *rest* of her life with him.

Kathy met Ray a short time after she and Benny parted ways. And thanks to Benny's sacrifice, she had found someone with strong arms to hold her through the pain of losing him. This was red-on-red passion that would, in the end, offer up a totally unexpected pain all its own; a hidden flame that, once exposed, would be severe enough to burn an already guarded heart.

Ray had, years before, fathered two children with his high school sweetheart and had since been married to and divorced from another woman in quite a short time. No doubt, Ray had been through pain of his own, but then, finally, he had met his match: a mellow, red woman with whom he could shun the bad memories and with whom he would create countless good memories. It was a decade plus they were all together in the small townhouse—Ray, Kathy, and the two dogs. Kathy had kept Benny's dog, Snapper (a miniature Schnauzer), and they got another hound dog named Beauregard together. They all spent many great years, and Ray's children were all grown up.

Happiness was fleeting though, as unbeknownst to Kathy, Ray re-kindled an old flame. Ray and the mother of his children were seeing one another, and Ray had secretly been taking their hound dog along to see her two young boys (of no relation to Ray). This went on for six months, at the end of which Ray told Kathy, on a whim, that he was taking the dog on a camping trip over the weekend. Kathy did not know as she was kissing him goodbye that in five minutes she would have a decision to make: to be ugly, or to be her kind, mellow self and hold the utmost composure.

Five minutes after Ray hit the road that Friday evening, Kathy got a call from a mystery woman, who introduced herself as Ray's high school sweetheart and the mother of his children. She confessed to Kathy that Ray had been seeing her—behind Kathy's back—for several months and that she knew Ray had no intention of leaving Kathy. My friend Katherine decided to play nice and discussed other niceties, including how attached her boys had gotten to their dog, Beauregard. Kathy decided to play along.

Ray played his part perfectly, calling the house on Sunday evening to ask, "Baby, can I pick up anything for dinner? I will be getting off the interstate soon!" Kathy welcomed her burly camping man into the living room and helped him get settled into the recliner. He pushed the lever, lounged back and rested his tired back. Beauregard played his part a little too well, laying over on the couch, his head on Kathy's lap, one tired pooch...that much was apparent.

Kathy asked Ray how the camping trip had gone and commented how "Johnny and Sam must have worn Beauregard clean out!"

Ray's eyes got as big around as silver dollars. He pulled

the lever, straightened himself in the chair, eyebrows raised like a cartoon character, and asked Kathy to repeat the words she had just spoken. There were no laughs that night. Kathy, disheartened, sent Ray on his way and told him that he could not live with her and get away with *that*.

Kathy and I shared many laughs over the awkwardness and unbelievable circumstances of this predicament. And when my friend speaks of Ray there is still a kindness there, though I don't understand how. Perhaps a part of her knows that he wounded himself just as much as he wounded her. It now occurs to Kathy that maybe he initially reconnected with Mystery Woman in an attempt to repair damage caused by a past broken home and fix the strained relationships with his children, all the while blindly destroying the warm home that Kathy and Ray had built for themselves. It had been the warmest home either of them had ever known.

As calm and cool as Kathy was toward Ray that Sunday evening, she did not sleep at all that night, nor many other countless nights to follow. "My soul cried each night as I slept. And I was forced to stare upon a face wracked with pain each morning." She entrusted this to me, and as she did, I could still see the pain behind her eyes as we spoke. Though the despair remained as a blackness over her for about a year, her stay in the dark cellar felt like an eternity.

While the hard glass of a bottle offers protection from the elements, if a wine stays closed off for too long, its attributes will erode with the years. There is a right time to crack open a bottle of wine, and that time was very nearly approaching! The light shining between the cellar doors may just have been a dinner date.

This date offered a glimmer of hope to a woman that had not been on a first date in thirteen years. Kathy had a single date with John, a trusted friend and a kind-hearted man who would, only a week later, discover that he was about to enter into a season of life that one would not wish upon any soul.

Kathy had known John for years as a former co-worker, and over the years they had become quite fond of one another. Through scattered conversations, she learned John had also been through hard times, and across the dinner table he revealed a bit more, lamenting how he had recently been divorced from his wife of 30 years. He and Kathy offered one another a shoulder to lean on.

The kiss they shared in her doorway following their single dinner date was a light that shone into the darkness, welcoming a new period of life for Katherine and illuminating a beautiful face. In her eyes was a faint glimmer of hope.

Not a week after their date, John was confronted with dreadful news: his ex-wife was about to begin a battle with terminal cancer. Loyally, John returned to his sick wife, remarried his bride, and ushered her over the threshold of death.

We may never know the value of our helpfulness to others.

We may never be able to glean what clarifying glimpses our lamps lend to the lives of our friends.

Up a few steps, Kathy had made the journey back into the light, and in her own words:

"A year to the day of when I sent Ray away—I met Glen!"

sparkling in the glass

Wine appears so lovely when it is swirled in the glass. Oh, to take a red lady dancing and never let her feet grace the floor!

If we are candid with ourselves, deep down we have all wished to play our part in a fairytale. As men we may dream of kneeling down and fitting a glass slipper to the delicate foot of a woman we love and cherish, while a woman waits for her prince to offer up his arm and escort her onto the ballroom floor. And together, we all desire to waltz in great circles through the night, and to one day scratch the words *Happily Ever After* at the bottom of a page.

You may have heard the saying, "You can take the girl outta the country, but you can't take the country outta the girl!" A country girl's fairytale reads a bit differently: a first meeting is not all shooting stars and fireworks, but instead affirms a hand-in-glove level of genuine comfort. On their first date, Kathy and Glen (meeting at a restaurant for some good country cooking) hugged one another's cheek like they had done it a thousand times before. Glen was a blonde-haired country boy with a full face, kind, blue eyes, and the most wonderful smile. Just days later, he invited Kathy to come "down home" to see where he lived and to meet his mother. Things progressed quickly from there; a whirlwind story of boy meets girl! It seems that this boy had made up his mind that Kathy was, and forever would be, *his* girl.

They continued to see each other fairly often. She loved being on the farm where he lived in Irvine, Kentucky. As you know, she was a country girl herself, and within the third week the boy called her from his tractor and told her, "You are burning my head up!" I have joked with Kathy since and told her that, considering her red hair to be a burning flame, perhaps she is so drawn to passion because she just needs somewhere to burn!

Within the pages of a fairytale all a girl needs are flowers, hearts, and diamonds, and such was the persistence of a determined old country boy! Glen wanted to share his life with Kathy, and from the depths of her being all Kathy desired was a man she could trust to be true. Glen was an open book: he took Katherine back to his childhood home in Jackson County and back to Drip-Rock Baptist Church, where he walked her down beside the creek waters of his baptism. I wonder—did this trip to the church bring Kathy back in time, back to the Baptist church of her childhood?

The two of them took a walk into the woods, where they

carved their initials into an old tree that had "proud bark" in the shape of a heart. For all you city folks, this is a section of knotted bark in the perfect shape of a heart. I imagine Kathy had a few knots in her own heart as the two walked hand in hand, deeper into the woods, where Glen first told Kathy that he loved her! I imagine there were birch trees that day that shared in the emotions that Kathy and Glen exchanged. How long did they sit under the branches, drinking in one another's presence?

Turns out there were a lot of "firsts" with Glen. Somehow Kathy had never managed to receive roses from a man, until Glen. Somehow she had never been taken to church by a man, until Glen; he took her to a service one Sunday evening. There were other firsts just around the bend; it was too good to be true. And she found herself thinking that the clouds should have rolled in by now, masking her Happily Ever After in a haze of doubt. But, week after week, her soul continued to dance in her chest and the life of happiness that she had prayed for so fervently became a bright, rising light on the immediate horizon.

One evening before Christmas, Glen dropped in and told Kathy to get *all dolled up*: "We are going dancing!" he exclaimed. In the car on the way there, he stirred up a heart-felt conversation garnished with the promise of a fancy new bracelet for Christmas. He made a slight detour and walked her into a jewelry store, where he immediately addressed the man behind the counter. "Please show us the rings…the sky is the limit!" he said, such as the sky *was* the limit of his love for Kathy. As their eyes met over the top of the jewelry case, serendipitously, their shared gaze settled down upon the same ring. It was an unconventional choice of ring, perfect for the pairing the two had become. The ring—to be her engagement ring—had a wide band of interlaced white and yellow gold. Numerous diamonds sparkled on her finger like the warm sunlight she felt shimmering on the surface of her heart. And so the red lady danced one of the most memorable nights of her life away.

That was Christmas 2006. In January 2007, Kathy suffered a massive heart attack.

Boy meets girl. Boy loves girl. Boy is scared to lose girl.

Kathy mentioned to me that it was indeed the heart attack that pulled back the reins of her fairytale carriage. And although Kathy does not doubt there was true purpose in her and Glen's lives becoming intertwined, she admits that the entanglement of their lives did not seem to reveal the purposes for which she had prayed. Kathy and Glen—though still together from 2005 through 2010—had turned down a road that would not lead them to "the ball." And so, it seemed, her sparkling glass heels would not grace the grand ballroom floor. Magical spell broken, the clock had struck midnight on the night of January 7th.

We are now getting closer and closer to the words that Kathy voices to me on a daily basis: words that often remind me that "God always goes before us to prepare the way."[1]

sweet mellow red

A delectable red for every day with aromas and flavors of lush, dark fruits. Wonderfully well-balanced, with a sweet finish.

I first met Katherine in downtown Louisville, in February of 2008. Her heart episode had not been enough to coax her toward the bright lights of "the other side;" rather, she was a wine about to be poured from the bottle and into the open air of a wide-rimmed glass.

Kathy met me as a young man soon after starting my first job—straight out of college.

I was young and green, and though the fruits of my new career were just beginning to bud, I found myself in a place of personal vulnerability, having recently ended a three-year relationship, and trying—the best I knew how—to balance a large amount of responsibility in my newly acquired position.

We both began work on a project to optimize our company's business processes, allowing for transition to a newly purchased computer system. The Project, though technical in nature, promised a colorful bouquet of experiences, working with professionals both young and old, of all different nationalities and temperaments.

As a young male, I honestly first noticed the bold variety of young women, all with their own blend of features, with accents that made them equally as enticing. Most of the young women flew in to fill contracted positions that kept them returning for work at the beginning of each week for up to two full years. Every weekend they would book return flights, back to their homes in the States, though many were born and raised abroad. I remember their faces like it was yesterday: there was the tall, slender African beauty with bronze skin from the Ivory Coast; the short, petite Indian with wavy black hair and a bright smile—a fountain of youthful exuberance— and how could I forget the blonde from Texas, with piercing blue eyes, that with a sideways glance could burn a hole clear through a young man's heart without her ever knowing it. I never dared step too close to that blue fire!

Lucky for me, it was only six short months between relationships before I found myself a home-grown Kentucky girl with a quick wit and a face full of radiant features! I saw in her eyes a silent promise that "never a dull moment" would be spent in her company. Her family offered me the sense that I had known them a lifetime: a divinely-tailored fit that would just as surely embrace my children as we began to offer one another a growth of intertwined support. Family is beautiful when it grows this way—when you just know you are meant to experience life together, and each moment confirms those feelings one after the other.

A person's work—an integral part of their life—is grand when their work community is able to offer support in much the same way. I have found tremendous value in the relationships that I built with my co-workers during The Project (that we still refer to as "The Project," though we have worked on several other projects since).

Kathy joined The Project team in mid-2007, before I was hired on myself, and she did not ask but told Glen where her work would be taking her: she would drive back and forth between Lexington and Louisville on the weekends and stay at a hotel during the week. She endured this frantic schedule because she knew of the job opportunities that would present themselves following The Project. Her contribution to The Project spanned close to three years, for all of which she wore an engagement ring on her delicate finger. I remember walking through and seeing a picture of a kind-looking man displayed on Katherine's desk, and I remember being glad that she had someone who truly cherished her. But despite his affections for her, Glen began to hold her at a distance following the heart attack. It was truly fear that increased that distance, not the extra eighty miles into the city of Louisville.

Following the implementation of our Project work, we

were all organized into post-project support teams, and it was amazing to me how close we had grown in that intensive, high-pressure atmosphere. Laughter had proven to be the best remedy for the stress; it had bound us all together, and it had allowed us to accomplish something great. Shortly after the initial implementation—when Kathy had moved back to a desk in Lexington—each individual, post-project support team embarked on Team Outings—more of a "thank you," I suppose, for a job well done. Kathy's team took a tour of Elk Creek Vineyard, and it was there at the winery, during a wine tasting, where she was nicknamed "Sweet Mellow Red" by one of our co-workers! It made perfect sense to me after I read the description of the wine after which she was named. I kept calling her this long after everyone else dropped it from use.

The description on the wine bottle, labeled "Sweet Mellow Red," read: *A delectable red for every day with aromas and flavors of lush, dark fruits. Wonderfully well-balanced, with a sweet finish. The perfect way to spread holiday cheers.*

Often when you think back on certain memories, they are fuzzy around the edges—a bit like dreams, and yet there is an unmistakable quality beneath them, suspending them just above the realm of "the natural". Tracing our memories backward, one into another, we encounter shadows of depth that can be felt but never seen in their full brilliance of color. Words fall short of memory.

The last Thanksgiving that Kathy spent with her father

was shared at Billy Ray and Charlotte's home in Brodhead, 2009. Glen sat at the table—following dinner—with his mother Carrie, his Aunt Faye, his Uncle Dean, and Katherine.

Kathy looked toward her daddy, leaned back in the recliner, hands behind his head, with a proud look on his face—eyes averted—as he listened intently to Dean tell him things he already knew to be true. Dean spoke of her intelligence, winning personality, and how proud he was just to *know* her and ended by saying he would claim Kathy for his own daughter if he could. As he spoke, Faye's head nodded in agreement. Unbeknownst to Katherine, these two—Faye and Dean—would months later offer her very loving support following her father's battle with diabetes, leading to kidney failure in the spring of 2010. If only Kathy had known those holidays to be his last.

Later, on that Thanksgiving afternoon, standing over her father in his easy chair, she voiced the word "goodbye" down to meet him, with all the care and love that her voice carries in it.

"If it weren't for your voice, I would not even know it was you," he responded. This was the point at which Kathy began to realize that her father's time on earth was waning. She explained to me that at this point, he could see shadows of things, but not necessarily the dimension and color.

After her father's passing (and after Katherine and I had reached a certain level of comfort with one another), she and I would sit back to back in the Lexington office over cups of steaming coffee, where she spoke careful words to me. Words relaying a vision of dimension and color that her daddy *was* able to behold as he lay dying, a shadow of things that those of us on earth are rarely able to glimpse.

I have enjoyed listening to a recording of Kathy's voice, over and over again, telling of the detailed visions that her father shared with his family just days prior to his death:

As he was dying at home—just a few days before his death— he experienced lots of things that give witness to where we know he is today, and, um, he called Mother into the room and said, "You're going to have to get these birds out of here!" And Mother asked, "What kind of birds?" and he said "Big. Huge. Birds." And he said, "Their wings are making lots and lots of noise." Mother went on to ask, "What color are these birds?" and he said, "They're white." She went on, "Well, where are they and I will get them out of your room." And he said, "They are all around my bed and I can't hardly see you because they have you surrounded. You are surrounded by *them." And so my mother, being the person she is, knew the time was near for my dad to go home.*

But he gave one more witness before that time occurred. And that was that Mother, sleeping next to a baby monitor, went into the other room where the receiver was, next to the hospital bed where Daddy lay. Anyways, she heard him restless in there, or whatever, so she went in there to see if he needed anything. And he was mad. Mother softly inquired, "Well, what's wrong?" and in an agitated tone he said, "They threw me back down here in the dirt; I did not want to come back down here!" *and she asked,* "Well, where did they throw you back down in the dirt from?" *And Daddy said that he had been to Heaven and that he had seen babies.* "I saw my mom and dad, and I saw babies," *he had said.*

When Katherine's mother asked how many babies he had seen, he answered, "Two." Kathy reminded me that both her momma and her older sister had lost their firstborn sons at birth; both were stillborn. "And so," Kathy explained, "we assumed, from the telling of his experience, that he had seen his son and grandson in Heaven."

I imagine the words of peace that Kathy voiced to her momma and sister upon the retelling of this sacred vision. I like to imagine the look on their faces the next time they stood shoulder to shoulder and visited Kevin Boone and Russell James in the church cemetery.

Kathy continued, matter-of-factly, that her daddy, being a "macho" man, had attempted to describe the beauty of what he had seen. *Pink,* Kathy pointed out, was definitely not something he would have spoken of, nor would he have described it as being *beautiful.* But there he lay, telling her mother Charlotte how "the shades of pink were absolutely magnificent," and that he "couldn't believe how beautiful it was" and that he "just really didn't want to come back *down here.*"

In a shaky voice, holding back a tear, Kathy confirmed to me that the Lord knows they have told this story, that she and her mother believe her father's visions to be a witness of where he has gone, and that they both believe they will see him again.

And so, as wine breathing in the glass, sweet and mellow aromas escape the sphere of her witness and fill the room with a *knowing* of something beyond.

breathe

Oh, the breath of a red wine as it lingers in the room! The reaches of its healing are unknown, and its grace is sure.

Tracing her memories backward, Kathy now takes us to an evening church service at Greenbriar Baptist Church in Irvine, KY, 2006.

Glen walked with Kathy on his arm, straight down the center aisle, to the very front pew on the right. There were only two rows of wooden pews in the small, country church, and as he escorted Katherine his face held a confident grin—as if he had just won the biggest prize at the county fair!

Following the service is when Kathy was first introduced to Faye and Dean. Faye admitted years later that she had thought, based on appearances, that Katherine was "uppity" (citified, and most likely a snoot). Based on appearance alone, this would have been an easy error to make, as Kathy is always well dressed, with nails done, and often gets compliments on her wardrobe and fine shoe selection. Humble beginnings, however, have never left this "city girl," and a haughty hair cannot be found on her red head.

Over time, Kathy breathed her calming words over Glen, telling him that though he had not been to church in several years, the walls and ceiling would not collapse in on him. Somehow, she gave Glen the confidence to march straight down the center to the front of that church and to know that he didn't have to worry himself with being "good enough" to earn grace, least of all the grace of any *person* in that place. After all, on his arm was Kathy—an open-handed bloom of grace and generosity. And generosity, like grace, is a flower of unmerited petals, and both are firmly rooted in love. Kathy revealed the very same flowering of love to Faye, softening her first impressions, and touching the heart of a lady in pursuit of answers.

About a year after her daddy passed, Katherine lost her new, surrogate father, Dean, to an accident involving a large lawn mower turning over on top of him and pinning him to the ground. His death was not immediate, and Dean lingered unconscious for a few hours after. Faye's question to her friend was, "He can't die, can he?" Katherine's response was gentle, but not gracious…"Yes, he can."

As you read these words, I know that you as a reader may well feel a more empty grief than Kathy or I have felt in such moments. Though it was hard on Kathy for the sake of Faye, Kathy and I both intimately know a presence that is imperceptible until it has been visited upon you:

Pathos.

I was first introduced to this word by the late poet John O'Donohue. The closest common word that he links pathos with is *absence*, and absence is most real when you lose someone that you love deeply: "Absence is not emptiness or vacancy, but it's the other side of presence."[1]

O'Donohue—an Irish poet and philosopher—comforted many people and families touched by the hand of death. As a Catholic priest for many years, he later became a poet and has left us with these deciphering words:

"In a certain sense, the beauty of grief after a person dying is about their new there-ness now in the invisible mode of absence. And it takes a long time after a person has died to actually develop a trust in their presence now in your life, in invisible form. The only difference between us and the dead is that we are visible—to each other and to ourselves—but that they now live *invisibly*, but that they're all around us."[2] The death of a loved one sets us on a new path, toward a new territory of spirit, introducing us to an invisible world that has been there all along.

For me, this new path began with the abrupt loss of my older brother, a story for a different time. I lost my brother during the same month that Kathy lost her father. Such a loss leaves a hole in you, one that clearly reveals a missing part—some part that can never be filled but that may only be fulfilled through deeper love.

As O'Donohue so eloquently phrases it,

"Pathos is the poignance that awakens in our hearts in the presence of loss."[3]

And so it is that *pathos* calls for the awakening of deeper parts of ourselves, shedding its light into any darkened corners when we allow it.

Kathy and I, during this season of our lives, often sat in deep conversation, and at night my own thoughts roared, compelling me to write them out. After reading the words that I had written to honor my brother, Kathy is the one that, in the midst of her own loss, still had enough grace to encourage me, praising the efforts of my writing. Many are the discussions we have had, and many pages of mine she has read. My gift to her is that I may help piece together the brilliance of color and beauty that our conversations have brought to me.

How different might my life have become if I had not had Katherine to breathe a sweet, mellow, and red graciousness into my life?

We all need friends such as this. We all need to become friends such as this.

I am glad that after the night of Kathy's heart attack, she remained on this earth to linger and to bless. On that January night in 2007, she sat up in bed, late in the evening, with a strange *knowing* of what was occurring, and voiced a simple prayer: "*Dear Lord, I need your help.*" The Lord took her by the hand and helped her up out of the bed and down a flight of thirteen stairs to unlock the door for the paramedics—and when the ambulance team could not wedge the stretcher through the door, she walked down the front steps, refusing any help—other than what she received from above—and laid herself back against the cold sheets of a stretcher, knowing she would be fine.

Following an operation to relieve the blockage, the report from the doctor was that she had experienced a one hundred-percent blockage of the main artery leading away from her heart. What is more, there was no visible damage to the heart muscle! In my mind, her presence here, now, is one hundred percent an "act of God," and she and I both believe that she has remained here to serve as a witness to the lives of some, to bless the lives of others, and to continue breathing on the world with her easy grace and with each and every beat of her blessed heart!

As I first finished drafting Katherine's story in 2015, five years had passed since the death of her father and of my brother, and it had been four years since the death of Dean. Faye had passed away earlier that year, in 2015, after a battle with an aggressive cancer of the colon, and another good friend of Kathy's was battling cancer of a different kind. One of her longtime friends and co-workers (that had often sat with us in Lexington) also said goodbye to her young son after several years of his battling colon cancer. Kathy was able to offer that friend great tenderness in her time of need. And yet another one of our co-workers was diagnosed with cancer and, thankfully, seemed to be winning his bout…perhaps due to the light of prayer that his loved ones lifted up into each and every black night.

Wine is bottled poetry.[4]

Kathy's life is a breath of wine, a prayer, reaching to a different world—but adding sweetness into our own. I was humbled to hear that when Kathy sat in Faye's hospital room, at her bedside, she read Faye the first draft of the first section of my testament to her life (the early text presented in the section titled *Love Like Wine*). For Faye, the realization that someone existed in her life to offer a visible glimpse of invisible grace was, I am sure, a priceless gift to help ease a broken body and give gentle rest to a tired mind.

Kathy promised to come back and read her *more*—another piece that I had begun writing, but one that I was unable to finish prior to Faye's passing. Here is a short excerpt from *The Garden Within*, in memory of Faye and clearly applicable to the nature of our dear, red-headed friend:

I have recently begun to think of the Garden of Eden as the place where our temporal universe and the realm of the eternal converge. Thinking of the descriptions from the Bible that tell of Eden, a place where four rivers come together, lush and green and thriving with life, I like to imagine that two of these rivers (the Pishon and Gihon) were spiritual springs that have since quelled and that the Tigris and Euphrates rivers (the two that remain today) brought in the earthly waters. I imagine that perhaps the Garden once provided man with a place in which to encounter the heavenly realms, a middle ground with rich soil cultivated by spiritual waters, a ground upon which the true experience of God was in full bloom.

I believe our own spiritual cultivations, if they are true, can produce eternal gardens in which our friends, families, and loved ones may experience the goodness of God. Isn't this exactly how we have been taught to pray? "Thy kingdom come. Thy will be done in earth, as it is in heaven."[5]

I often love to sit and reflect on the times and the places that have represented "Eden" for me. Most of these memories involve elements of the natural world and also being in community with those whom I love most. Both nature and our loved ones are good at hiding us from the world and creating a "space" for us; they create for us places that time cannot touch, where the eternal is welcome and may become known. These spaces are heavenly gardens that are accessible from earth.

the vine and
the branches

*The wine that joins together all those sitting 'round
the table is a wine that stems from a branch of
the all-embracing Vine of Love.*

What is "God" but a three-letter word?

How can human language ever hope to touch who, or
what, God is? Is not "God" only our *name* for what we experience to be Divine in this life? Sure, we have sacred texts to
which we cling and that help give us guidance, but what are
these texts but stories of how ordinary people have encoun-
tered an extraordinary God?

Well, some of them not so ordinary, but fully human
nonetheless.

The person of Jesus, understanding the power that lies in
between the seams of a great story, left us a few great ones—
that is for sure.

Jesus was a carpenter-poet that fitted together a powerful
collection of parables that even today offers us the greatest

clarity and deepest insights into the true heart of "God." Ultimately, these parables, paired with stories accounting for His time here, offer us unforgettable icons of endless love—a portrait of what life should be. Through an examination of the elements in these parables, the transformations manifested by His miraculous acts of great love, and our own personal, human experience, we can only hope to become enfolded into a greater understanding and elevated awareness of *who* God is.

The well-known story that I often ponder is the Wedding Feast in Cana—the first miracle of Jesus.

This may as well be a story of time travel:

Jesus was at the high point of entertainment the people of that time would have taken part: a wedding. The company was great, the food was good, but the caterer had misjudged the crowd. The wine was now gone, and there was no corner market. The mother of Jesus thought this would be a good time to introduce the people to her son—Carpenter/Poet/Master Sommelier?

Jesus instructed a servant to fill empty wine pitchers with water and then dip some out and take it to the Head of the Banquet. There goes that servant's job, right? Nope. Turns out that the wine Jesus had fermented was better than the first, "choice" wine. And while most people would have served the best wine first, Jesus had apparently saved the best for last; wine that was anything but watered down. Six stone jars of water, holding 20-30 gallons each, were transformed into upwards of 120 gallons of wine.

OK—push "pause" real quick.

How convenient is that little button on our remote control…when we are watching a fantastic movie and don't want to miss the best part, but we've run out of refreshments? Out of the pantry we emerge, uncorking another bottle.

Not only did Jesus hit the proverbial pause button, but he might as well have traveled to 16th century France, or 18th century Spain, or 20th century Argentina. Jesus might as well have spent a few summers under the Tuscan sun!

On these theoretical travels, how long would it have taken Him to learn from some of the great wine makers the art of creating a formidable wine? And how many years could have been invested in crafting a truly exceptional vintage? And— outside of that—how long would this exceptional vintage need to sit in fermentation?

Here we are given a new name for God: The Vine, with branches that extend down through the ages. But, if we are being more simplistic and throwing out the notion of time travel, only a few seconds were needed for this *holy* fermentation, apparently.

Needless to say, in addition to the time required to make 120 gallons of wine, you would also need over 2,000 pounds of grapes! The weight of this realization is striking to me.

Who is He that stands outside of time?

Who is He that can craft wine without grapes?

This event in Cana of Galilee is one that should not be dismissed without deep reflection. I truly believe the hands involved in turning water into wine are at the very root of what has made my friend sweet and mellow...and red.

These are the same hands capable of transforming *any* life of ordinary water into a celebration of wine; a transfiguration based in our experiences, realized in the depths of our memories.

Perhaps Sweet Mellow Red was the vintage that Jesus served up that evening in Cana, but He called it by a different name. The name we would both know it by is *Katherine*.

The speaking of a single word is a powerfully creative act.

There is a reason God is able to speak to us through nature. The natural world is an extension of God, and we an extension of that world. What word did it all start with?

Sweet, Mellow, or Red?

What three words might He have spoken to call you into existence?

(Encouraging? Supportive? Embrace?)

The text in the first chapter of John reveals Jesus as the "Logos" (the Word), and this poem tells us that everything that has been created was created through the Word.

What word did it all start with?

The Christian view is that Jesus was both fully God and fully human. For me, this presents us a beautifully, painted stained-glass—a miraculous mosaic, Jesus being the Vine, each of us—the extended branches. If we remain in Him we bear fruit—the scriptures tell us[1]. The stained-glass fragments a multitude of shades, round purplish grapes.

There is a bit of pain involved, as leaves must be pruned, we see these in the brown, earth tones toward the bottom of the glass. But the harvest will be more bountiful for it, the wine more robust.

And here is the Word that started it all,

"And God said, Let there be *light*:"[2]

The human portrait becomes divine, in the Light that shines through.

[This is] the true Light, which lighteth every man that cometh into the world.[3]

round the table

Many great conversations happen 'round the table; many a sweet song 'round the hearth.

Strange how recent exchanges over coffee, scriptures that show up in my inbox, and the open ear of a wise friend remind me every day of just how sweet it is to have such a friendship. There is belonging here, but no room for judgment around our table.

Before I take my seat, any judgments of my friend's life must be assessed. Unforgiveness and compassion cannot sit at the same table, for compassion is the secret heart of forgiveness.

I remind myself that there can exist no judgment in forgiveness. And that this forgiveness begins as a personal endeavor of humility. We are—every one of us—flawed; but how much more beautiful does that make our embrace?

For those that believe only a "watered down" version of Christianity is being served here, that is not true. Kathy's life provides insights beyond scriptural sense, extending into the realm of spiritual experience. There is a deeper Love here that lives at the heart of a more *elemental* understanding of the God that created our universe.

True friendship is rare to find, but it *can* be found, and I am convinced that having an Anam Ċara (Gaelic for "soul friend") is the key to introducing balance into all aspects of our lives. Friends such as this act as mirrors, helping us to discover who we are as unique and ever-changing individuals. They reveal to us that we are indeed suspended within an invisible world of spirit. Such friendships are a visitation of pure Beauty upon our lives, and a deep spirituality lives in the heart of them; they are a Love Like Wine.

There is nothing quite so beautiful as a red velvet wine that generously splashes into empty glasses standing side by side. The first sip of such an essence wraps the heart in a warm, crimson robe.

The bread and the wine from the table's top are provisioned from the depths of body and blood. There is no greater love than this: as was portrayed when a purple robe was cast aside, clothing the heart of the world in compassion. As a glass was raised in the upper room, the words, "This [wine] is my blood"[1] poured from His lips, and those words covered us all. At its deepest heart, then, wine *is* love, and all wine flows from the one true Vine. Connected from within, we are sweet fruits that are being nurtured by one another as we become suspended in a blending of our spirits.

Our imaginations are powerful things:

Leaving the table now, I will sit with Kathy and her daddy, watching a small television screen. A moderately well-known episode of "I Love Lucy" pans across large round tubs and woven wicker baskets overflowing with the purple grapes of harvest time. At such festivals, the beautiful feet of women press down and release the juice from beneath the skins of the grapes, but as with any scene involving Lucy, the laughter is uncontainable as she inadvertently becomes enlisted to walk the wine vat. The look on her face as she feels the first grapes squish beneath her toes is priceless! It is a scene of such robust laughter…as Lucille Ball accidentally knocks a short Italian woman off balance, backward into the pool of juice! As things progress (and the laughs begin to roar), the two women begin throwing handfuls of mashed grapes at one another, staining their white garments in a violet splatter. The red juice offers such contrast against Lucy's fair skin and blonde curls.

The time has come for us all to put our feet down into the pool of juice. For me, this is not a picture of all the glamorous people that I have met in my lifetime, but instead of all the uniquely beautiful souls, man and woman and child that I share life with—I see the radiant faces of people I love dearly unified in a harvest celebration of great love.

It is of little wonder to me that the everyday elements of bread and wine should have been chosen as icons to join us all in belonging. Everyone is invited to our table—even if you have not labored in the vineyard and have yet to participate in the harvest, there is a glass for everyone and enough bread for all. Becoming one in love, we are all water being turned to wine.

What good are our experiences if they are unable to be rendered into drink; a drink that can be generously splashed into the empty glasses of our loved ones?

It is a bittersweet thing as I write these last few lines. My red-headed friend remains, and while I wish I had the foresight to envision the full impact that her life may have on this world (in a way I do), I feel her impact in each and every conversation that we have, and these feelings stir the faith in my heart. Like the feeling I got during a conversation we started just the other day…another vision from the rafters of her memory, framed into a poem:

into the deep

Up into the attic, she leads me stair by stair.
The darkened edges of her memory guide me.

On, to the back wall, something leans in the shadow.
A dust-filled, white sheet drapes down from both corners.

Just a little tug and the linen fans like a window curtain.
The light let through revealing a timeless, oil painting.

A man stepping off…into the deep, still clinging to a
swampy bank.
The dark tree beside him reaches upward; Spanish Moss
fleeces down.

Tugging at the opposite corner, a trusted bloodhound's
nose turns down.
Emerging from the murk of the water is the man's
soaked, flannel sleeve.

In his arm he cradles a matted pup; a companion for his
floppy-eared friend.
Light from the stained-glass, attic window gleams
against relief of kind, caring eyes.

The stanzas above I compiled from Kathy's recollection
of an old "country" sermon, the author of which is unknown,
now a song of memory—still whispered—at the hearth of my
friend's soul. For Kathy, the step down into "the deep" was a
step on down into the unsettled waters that only faith could
see her through. On the bank of the marsh, where this pas-
tor-hunter reaches down to rescue his beloved hunting dog's
companion, he has discarded both rifle and knapsack among
the tall reeds. For Kathy, it was only by laying down every
burden that she herself was able to become *arms of grace*.

a toast overlooking the vineyard

A high-tech toast—over text—can join hearts together just the same.

Upon dropping this manuscript into the hands of my friend, over a five-year journey came to an end. Though I had only been actively writing her story on and off for a couple of years, we both realized that the writing of our friendship had begun long ago.

The one true Author, who chose to write our stories so that we would sit back to back a couple days a week, was only just beginning to weave together the vines of a far more luminous story. A story within a vineyard that is much larger than we could ever imagine; one that we are all, including *you* as a reader, an intricate part of.

So what I include below is a "Toast over Text"—a toast that occurred via cell phone, over a short message service that allowed for us to record, in Kathy's words, a "toast in spirit." A toast in which we would like *everyone* to take part. So, whether you are drinking wine or drinking juice…such a toast provides a deep glimpse into what the light of true friendship may bring to our lives. Grab a glass!

Strike the call. Email me your response, so that years from now I can look back at your words! Afterwards, I may have to crack open an old vine zin to celebrate!!

Will do. I might have to crack open my old vine zin too. We can toast in spirit.

If you have not tried it, it is delicious!!!

Sent you an email. Let's open the bottle and celebrate!

Popping the cork in a bit, I will sit and read your email after I get my wife and daughter tucked-in!!

Let me know when you pop it, I will pop mine then too.

Old vine time?! I will count us down..

Ok have at it!

3.. 2.. 1.. pop!

Done
Pouring
Swirling
Tasting

Sweet Mellow and Red!

Exactly!

It has been a wonderful journey

Yes it has!

This toast is to you! Thank you so much for your endeavors that will forever be evident in black and white. But most of all the parts that remain in the heart and soul!

Clink

Your words here and in your email mean very much to me!! Clink right back!!!

I am blessed to have known you!

Ditto!!!! My friend. You know it is not often I become so "known" to another human.

You are my truest friend.

Ditto again. Your trueness is what made me comfortable enough to be really known.

I include the text messages above only as a window into a truly two-sided friendship that illustrates the true inspiration that this type of friendship may become. You are invited to the same table of friendship, so that you may experience the power of *being known* by another. When we allow ourselves to become known by others, we truly become known to ourselves...and on such a journey, we will most surely be shown glimpses of the God that created our universe and that has created *all* of us. He has great plans for each and every one of our lives!

A *chink* is the sound two glasses make when they are lightly tapped together and go their separate ways. A *clink* is the sound our glasses make this evening, as they are pressed together and held in repose. And the wine we drink—though poured from separate bottles—is a toast to the very same vintage: a Sweet Mellow Red. **There is an extra glass for _you_.**

True Love is indeed like a fine wine, and I am blessed to have known a Love that reaches across religion, beyond judgment, and into the true heart of Grace. This Love that I have come to know flows freely from the woman that I call Sweet Mellow Red.

I wish I could take credit as the sole author of this work, but there were times, as I sat suspended in waves of inspiration, that this writing experience felt more a "plagiarism of spirit," as words seemed to flow past me, through trembling fingertips, and fill the emptiness of a blank page.

Standing in the midst of the first showers of spring, I look again to the birch trees, bark darkened by the rain. I notice that the branches of the trees and others surrounding them have not yet been weighed down by the burden of leaf or berry. Quite a sight I see as the pale morning light stencils a silhouette of new growth and individuality against a canvas of urban stone.

God's hand is indeed in every season, and we are all divine objects of His immense Beauty.

Cheers, to the _sweet mellow red_ Love that has formed my friend into this portrait of Truth.

a letter from red

Electronic mail, offering us a well-penned letter of heart.

There has been some delay in my writing to you this evening. You are such a special person to me. My words I am sure will not surely convey the rainbow of emotions that the added chapters invoked upon my soul and spirit. Your perception of my life is such a gift that I can't describe. Talk about breathing life, you have done the same. I keep shaking my head and saying "WOW!" The description of my father's passing is so detailed and such a reminder that I will see him again! And the poem about the sermon was simply awesome! The dedication started the emotion and it went from there. I love how you describe there is room for everyone around the table. This is bigger than me and you, I believe! And the Garden piece in there brings back how I know Faye would have loved it so.

Bill, the leaving the table scene is profound in the fact that it gives the hope that we see our loved ones in another realm but also in our mind's eye on a daily basis and the comparison to the Lucille Ball episode gives a little comic relief. I love how you have woven the spirit of God throughout the whole story. I could not be who I am unless God had gone before me in all of these scenes of my life. The part about you losing Dave intertwined here is the proof that we, like the vines, are all intertwined with each other. I love that you let the reader know a little more about your story too and how your vine became intertwined with mine. This is the proof we need to know, that "God always goes before us to prepare the way."

You can't know what a gift you have bestowed!

Oh, and I do Love You!!!!! God has made you in his likeness and is not finished with either of us yet!

Thank you my Anam Ċara,

Red

a half-empty bottle of blessing

A half-empty bottle of blessing shall never pour its last, as blessing begets blessing.

Spring, summer, fall, and winter—the seasons of our lives. Each is comprised of many years and signature notes. I write these words in the summertime of my life, while each syllable stirs the autumn leaves in the blessed heart of Red. Though Katherine is well into the harvest time of her life, the winds of winter are no chill the warmth of her heart need yet contest.

The grapes have been harvested, the red juice matured, the cork has been twisted, the wine now poured. Glass after glass, blessings are served, and though the bottle appears half empty, by some miraculous cycle the level shows restored.

Blessings served and blessings returned—to hands that show the mark of age—I wish blessings to a lady with unchanging, auburn hair!

Her smile reveals the very heart of summer; she is a colorful portrait of autumn. But how does she keep those deep blue eyes grounded and maintain such a youthful, exuberant soul?

Her presence is a warm blanket of shelter for green, budding vines…blessings to her, this friend of mine, who has ushered me from amongst the cool showers of spring and into the warmth of summer.

Will we not *all* become known against the blessings that we bestow?

Dare *you* come nearer this vessel of love—a Sweet Mellow Red—trustable to pour its light into the unknown, unsheltered nights?

a sweet finish

The sweetness in a last sip of wine is the embrace of all that came before.

"Well, what ever happened with Glen?"

That question is the reason I have added this section. Glen still calls Kathy sometimes, asking, "Why did I ever let you get away, Babe?"

Kathy never has a good answer for him, and when he suggests she should drop on through Irvine sometime, Katherine says, "No, you'll have to come here if you want to see me."

They chat for a bit like old friends, then say their goodbyes.

Kathy has not closed off all the rooms of her heart. She has somehow managed to befriend her sorrows and to remain gracious in her patience.

She attended the funeral of Ray's mother; offered a hug to both Ray and his sweetheart. Both of them welcomed her; both were thankful for her presence.

I joined my friend at her home for lunch one day and walked up the front steps past weather-worn figurines of Snapper Lew and Beauregard—his hound dog companion.

When speaking with my good friend, we often pick

through the old stories of Aziz, but we have no need to only speak of the past. In recent years, Aziz has begun making annual business trips, and for several years he has made special arrangements to fly into Kentucky and take a drive with Kathy. Each time he visits they enjoy a nice home-cooked meal with Katherine's mother in Brodhead.

Friendship is as sweet an ending as any—it embraces all that came before.

Feelings of Love

Here is my heart
Take thee my gift
For I'll give it unto you

Timely gifts are unseen
My love for you is hidden
Search your soul and you may find it

Seasons in the sun are lost
One does not remember those times
Can they be re-lived?

Remember I'll love you always
You are all the reasons I need to live
Transplanted deep into my inner being is you

Here is my heart
For the asking, it is yours
For I'll give it unto you

—Katherine Rae
(Circa 1981)

new words
amongst friends

How *did* the words Being Known (and the words Anam Cara, for that matter) make it into this text? I had not even written those words into to the early draft that I handed Katherine on that Friday afternoon.

Only in her letter did Red mention these words to me; words that have been part of a dialogue that another of my "soul friends" and I began using some time ago...words that bled over into our conversations, not to mention into conversations with other friends of mine.

"Being Known" is actually a website (.org) that I built for close friend (and fellow author) Joshua Fraley. That was several years ago and at the time I had not written much of anything (other than the PHP web-coding for his new website). The first article that was posted to the site was this reflection of Josh's on one of the Psalms...but one I found so insightful that I told my friend we needed to build him a website around—a place where he could share his work. So, included in the next few pages is a short article titled "Being Known" that explores the depths of what it actually means to "know" God and that ultimately began my journey of investing in open, honest, and authentic friendships and the meaning that each of those friendships may hold!

Close to the end of Josh's *Being Known* article was my first introduction to John O'Donohue, a man that would have been more than welcome to join us in conversation at our table of friendship (were he still walking this earth). The late Irish poet and philosopher John O'Donohue has without a doubt provided me a *refreshed* view of the Christian faith. He has given me new words and language, with which to guide my thoughts toward the shore of "The Divine" (that other, more mysterious name for God; a new name that does not put a limit on the Divine Imagination that *was* before the creation of this world).

Who would have thought that simply changing the name that I used to refer to God could lead me down a road of discovering the enormity of the hand that set into motion the fluency of the Cosmos?

Calling someone a close friend would not do either it seemed…in his book "Anam Cara" (Gaelic for Soul Friend), O'Donohue has done much the same thing for me—breaking down walls of old language and freeing the *notion* of what great friendships may potentially become.

Language is so important. It allows us to reach over and across to one another.

At some point in time Josh and I transitioned from calling Being Known "his website" to calling it "our website" and we have since begun entertaining the idea of inviting new authors to post their stories to the site: **www.beingknown.org**. Offering people a forum, we wish to allow them to share their stories and in doing so, find new places to "become known" by others. We invite you to share your stories of authentic love—derived from the depths of experience and relationship—that will truly change the world.

You are invited to share your story by contacting us through the "ABOUT" section of the website.

The first story that I shared on beingknown.org was the story of my older brother, Dave, and the impact that his life had upon mine. The *writing* of that story—A Texas Tune—changed my life, as did the *response* I received from those that also love my brother. The sharing of such Love allows for the entanglement of our vines, and as we grow, we grow into one another; the result is beautiful! Within the heartfelt conversations we engage in with one friend we gain warmth to offer, as comfort, for another friend who may sit in a time of isolation.

Here is my friend Joshua's reflection on Psalm 139 that has altered my ideas of what it actually means to know God:

Being Known

A REFLECTION ON PSALM 139
(Written By: Joshua Fraley)

Psalm 139 is a beautiful psalm, and it begins, "O Lord, you have *searched* me and *known* me" (NASB). The psalmist goes on to suggest that his entire life is intimately known to God, that he is, in some way, enveloped by God. Although the language of the entire psalm is poetic and the content is deep, what is most striking about this passage is that the very experience of being intimately known was an incredibly encouraging experience for this individual. Surely the psalmist, like the rest of us, had all sorts of vulnerabilities, sins to hide and gifts to stash away, yet the simple awareness that his creator could see right through him brought him a tremendous amount of comfort. I think there is something incredibly special and spiritually healthy about being transparent—that is to say, being open to being known.

It's no secret that people find it difficult to be open with others. Phrases such as "intimacy issues" get thrown around a lot in our culture, and professionals have connected these types of issues with all sorts of other problems in society. Science, however, is not the only facet of our culture that is aware of the problem. This issue is repetitively used in the entertainment industry. Sitcoms and other comedies often place their characters in uncomfortable social situations where transparency, often between men, is a humorous theme. We laugh because we understand exactly how awkward those experiences can be. Sadly, what modern entertainment does not communicate very well is that they are in fact missed spiritual opportunities.

Religion has always had something to say about our natural tendency to be closed off. For 2500 years the Buddhists and the Hindus have philosophically and psychologically been trying to point humanity to the notion that humans are interconnected, and the healthiest way to live is aware of and open to that fact. For this reason, compassion for all other living things has always been a central religious tenet in the East. Compassion, of course, literally means "to suffer with," and is an activity that requires a certain amount of intimacy, even if that intimacy is *felt* more than it is intellectually grasped. The religions of the Middle East also address the issue. Judaism, in particular, has maintained an intense focus on family, social life, and the theological notion of covenant that may be at least three to four thousand years old. Jewish theology and historical experience compels individuals to see themselves as part of an intimate community traveling through human history together; circumstances are secondary to the goal of maintaining such a community. Generally speaking, open relationships with God and man, is one of the greatest goals of most all of the world's religions.

For those of us who claim to be Christian there is a very clear calling to intimacy and openness. Jesus prayed to his father, "I do not ask on behalf of these alone, but for those also who believe in me through their word; that they may all be one; even as you, Father, are in me and I in you, that they also may be in us, so that the world may believe that you sent me" (John 17:20-21). There are at least three very clear points in Jesus' prayer: 1) Christians are called to be one with each other, 2) Christians are called to be one with the Father and Son, and 3) the Father's chosen method of convincing the world of Jesus' validity rests in the *human* demonstration of these relationships. It would seem that Christians who are generally closed off are hardly "Christian" at all.

A central question is: "What sorts of things would a spiritually healthy Christian open himself up to?" What does Jesus' prayer look like in every day life? I believe that the scriptures point to several general types of intimate relationships that are the substance of spiritual health. I further believe that these relationships are frequently seen in individuals who have acquired deep spiritual lives which are evident throughout history.

Psalm 19 illustrates two of these relationships quite clearly. The entire psalm has two dominant themes. The first is the natural world, and the second is the "Law of the Lord." In his introduction the psalmist claims, "The heavens are telling of the glory of God; and their expanse is declaring the work of His hands. Day to day pours forth speech, and night to night reveals knowledge." As the psalmist continues he points out that nature, the weather patterns, the seasonal cycles, the heat and the cold, truly does reveal God to human beings. Although most Christians would agree with this, the pace of modern culture has so distracted the majority of the population that people have almost no real *experience* of nature itself. In an intellectual way Christians are happy to point out that there must be a God because of the complexity of the created order, yet the closest these individuals will get to that complexity is observing it in a documentary. But this simply cannot be the type of knowledge the psalmist is talking about. He suggests that for such intimate knowledge, "There is no speech, nor are there words; their voice is not heard." Relationship with nature is not an intellectual pursuit that can be described audibly or intellectually. It is an intimacy that comes from direct experience.

The second theme of Psalm 19 points us toward a relationship with the "Law of the Lord." The psalmist states, "The Law of the Lord is perfect, restoring the soul; the testimony of the Lord is sure, making wise the simple. The precepts of the Lord are right, rejoicing the heart" (7-8). What could be spiritually more healthy than a rejoicing heart and a restored soul? But there is a difficulty for many of us in this passage. For the psalmist, certainly an ancient Hebrew, the "Law of the Lord" must imply the whole religion of his day. It was not simply the sacred texts (Law of Moses) and the scrolls they were written on as modern people imagine the "Law of the Lord" to be. It included the *practice* of the ethical laws as they related to other people, the sacrificial laws that governed correct behavior at the temple, and purification laws that governed personal behavior and rituals. What the psalmist is pointing to is the fact that his "religion" restored his soul.

Many people today are weary of the term "religion," and seem to prefer the pursuit of "spirituality" alone. The term "religion," however, simply comes from a Latin root word that means "to tie, fasten, or restrain," and it means this in a conscientious sense. The idea is that "religion" is repetitive behavior that is supposed to make people meticulously aware of their conscience, which in turn allows them to live in a proper way. This is why the psalmist is so content with his religion. Most people who believe they are living in the proper way are, in a spiritual sense, happier people. The challenge for modern Christians is to be open to religious environments. For those of us who would complain that Church is boring, theologically confused, or scientifically ignorant, it still remains a workhorse for spirituality and can truly be an incredible framework for the restoration of our souls.

Returning to John 17 and Jesus' prayer, the most obvious relationships that create a healthy spiritual life are human relationships and relationship with God. As far as the former is concerned, on the surface it would appear as if most people

are in a tremendous amount of relationships with other people. The majority of modern individuals are busy at work or
school anywhere from forty to sixty hours a week, roughly
at least one third of their lifetime. But those two places are
hardly enriched with openness and intimate knowledge, which
require a tremendous amount of *qualitative* communication.

One of my favorite statements about the nature of qualitative communication was made by an Irish poet who was
asked what it was like to experience the beauty of God in daily
life. He replied,

"One way, and I think this is a really lovely way, [is to ask
yourself a question]. And the question is: 'When is the last
time that you had a great conversation?' a conversation which
wasn't just two intersecting monologues, which is what passes
for conversation a lot in this culture. But when did you have
a great conversation in which you overheard yourself saying
things that you never knew you knew. That you heard yourself
receiving from somebody words that absolutely found places
within you that you thought you had lost and a sense of an
event of a conversation that brought the two of you on to a
different plane.... a conversation that continued to sing in your
mind for weeks afterwards ... I've had some of them recently,
and it's just absolutely amazing, as we would say at home, they
are food and drink for the soul, you know?"[1]

If I were honest, I would admit that I am not sure if I have
had a conversation recently that was "food and drink for the

soul." Culture has become inundated with social networks, cell phones, and emails, all intended to connect individuals, but instead has created a sort of watered down version of friendship. Current communication is industrial, fast, efficient, and cheap, and most folks would be hard pressed to remember even one conversation that served their soul in this way.

Our communication problem renders Jesus' commandment to his disciples, "Love your neighbor as yourself" (Matt 22:39), a nearly impossible task. We refuse to spend more energy communicating, and the forthcoming generations will not even know how. Even if they want to love someone the way they know they would desire to be loved, they will not be equipped with enough experience to do so, or a long enough attention span to begin to touch the issues in a deep, personal way. Honest, open communication, whatever it may look like in the moment, must be safeguarded by modern Christians.

Finally, a brief word about intimacy with God: "O Lord you have searched me and known me." All the other relationships in my life, nature, religion, and friendship, must culminate in and serve as indicators of knowing and being known by God. Depending on who is asked the question, the process of knowing God can seem complex, practically and intellectually, but it is most simply understood when it is viewed in light of the other three. An intimate relationship with God can spring from the awe and inspiration experienced in nature, the restraint and self control preached by religion, and the deep affection and selfless relationship of true friendship. In all three cases the famous statement made by John the Baptist before he was executed applies, "He must increase, but I must decrease" (John 3:30). Nature, religion, and friendship should, in a positive sense, make us feel small. They are excellent preparation and paths for the experience of a God that is infinite love. Our ego must begin to shrink in order for us to experience Him. That is certainly why the psalmist's experience of God was not just deep, but so enveloping that it seemed as if he was transparent before God, completely seen and known. He had the distinct feeling of being "closed in behind and before" (5), like a drop of water in the ocean.

There are many reasons why humans remain closed off to the most significant experiences in life, why they refuse to be transparent. Among those reasons pride always stands at the front, followed closely by time limitations. Transparency, however, dissolves pride and allows frailty and fault to be seen, and our time must simply be reprioritized. Whether we are aware of it or not, I think we all crave the peace and satisfaction that follow from intimacy with God. In our worst moments, we would love to be able to join the psalmist and proclaim with confidence, "If I say surely the darkness will overtake me, and the light around me will be night, even the darkness is not dark to You, and the night is as bright as the day. Darkness and light are alike to you... lead me in [this] everlasting way" (11-23).

acknowledgements

Thank you, most of all to God, the one true God that cannot be contained in any of the simple images that we paint in our minds, or in the wealth of words that leave our tongues. Thank you for the awe of this world.

Thank you, Katherine, for openly sharing the colors of your life and the depth of your experiences with us. Your life is a portrait of Beauty!

Thank you to my wife, Mel, and to my children for providing for me *daily* frame points of love, inspiration, support, and consistency; a golden frame for my brush strokes to inhabit.

Like my friend I, too, have deep roots fastened firmly in the rich soil of a loving family. Thank you to my family: Mom and Pops, Brett and Cindy, Sarah and Dan, Lori and Chad and to my older brother Dave. We all look forward to sitting round the table with our Buddy D (when we move beyond this life).

In regard to a growth of intertwined support, a BIG thank you to my mother-in-law, Kari! Thank you for caring for my children. I most surely would not have the freedom (or energy) to write were you not there helping us in more ways than we can count! Thanks to my father-in-law, Chuck, for being a great friend and for having a kind comment for each of my blog posts.

I look to the future as my life becomes more and more intertwined with wonderful people that have accepted me into their family: thank you to Dan and Amanda, Kimmie and Dave, and to Dave Gr. and Rachel. What a great family my wife has surrounded me with.

To all of my friends that I call Anam Cara: in sitting at the table of your friendships I have discovered a Eucharist, a love-feast of Holy Communion that offers nourishment to my soul. Because of your love, while there is famine all around, I remain fed.

Without friends and family my attempts at writing would be unrefined; broad strokes at a slack canvas. Thank you to all of you for your influence into the richness of my life!

To Joshua Fraley, the first of my Soul Friends: the Mediterranean shore (that I imagined running along in the prologue of this book) was an image from the world brought to life in your book *To See Like Marcion*. Thanks for a truly inspiring read that brought me back to a world where religion was a bit younger, and mythology was prevalent among the old-world cultures. For me, you have somehow underscored the importance of the *quality and character* that we should bring to the altar of our existence in current times. I still don't know how you pulled off such a captivating read! You have my envy! Thank you for your counsel as a fellow writer, and for your help with my dreadful habits of bad grammar...thanks for all the conversation, thanks for your friendship, and thanks for allowing me to include (as an afterword) your reflection on Psalm 139.

Thank you to the late John O'Donohue—my Irish poet friend—whose book *Anam Ċara* has given me a name for the deep friendships that "people" the inner landscape of my life. And to Krista Tippett, for her On Being podcast entitled "The Inner Landscape of Beauty" (Krista's interview with O'Donohue has served as a great introduction to a uniquely beautiful soul! How I wish I could have met him while he was here!) Also, I will say that John O'Donohue's *Wisdom from the Celtic World* (Sounds True audio series) has forever altered the language that I use to meet the "wild danger" of the Divine Presence. Books and audio are all available at www.johnodonohue.com.

Thank you also to Elk Creek Vineyards for providing me a truly brilliant name for my red-headed friend! Though the vintage of "Sweet Mellow Red" is not always available, Elk Creek continues to offer a large selection of both reds and whites.

A big thanks to all the Kentucky wineries that are gracious enough to sell my book!

Thank you, oh so very much, to the early readers of my drafts and for your most-cherished feedback: David, Deborah, Tony, Gaye, Chad, Sue, Kim, Sarah, Donna, Dani, and (of course) Kathy and Josh.

A special thanks to Dani, for your copy and line edits, and for your amazing proofreading skills—that have truly transformed this work into something I am proud of. I am humbled by your gift with words.

The cover for this book is a watercolor, painted by my 80-year-old artist friend, Mr. William Tippie. I have become a big collector of WT's work and he has become one of my all-time great friends. Thanks very much to the "other" Bill!

Thanks to David Provolo, for a great job with interior and cover designs. If you are searching for a book designer, look up this man's work on Reedsy and you will be impressed!

Last, but certainly not least, thanks to my primary editor, Kylie Roberts. This was a truly organic experience, and I was amazed by your patience and willingness to help these pages in retaining my voice. Thank you for helping to add greater depth and fluency to this work. I feel a rooted depth, in the friendship that we have built over coffee and donuts each week, and I most certainly recommend your friendship (and editing services) to anyone!

For editing inquires of your own you may reach Kylie at: askkylie.com.

In closing, I will say again that True Love is indeed like a fine wine, and I am blessed to have known a Love that reaches across religion, beyond judgment, and into the true heart of Grace. This Love that I have come to know flows freely from the woman I call Sweet Mellow Red—**thank you to that Love**.

end notes

Chapter 7: Down into the Cellar

1. Emily Dickinson, Letters from Dickinson to Mary Bowles, Spring 1862. "The Heart wants what it wants - or else it does not care".

Chapter 8: Sparkling in the Glass

1. Holy Bible (Paraphrasing from King James Version), Deut. 31:8.

Chapter 10: Breathe

1. John O'Donohue, Wisdom from the Celtic World: The Divine Imagination (Disc 3, Track 4, 1:54), Sounds True (www.soundstrue.com) 2005.

2. John O'Donohue, Wisdom from the Celtic World: The Divine Imagination (Disc 3, Track 6, 1:43), Sounds True (www.soundstrue.com) 2005.

3. John O'Donohue, Wisdom from the Celtic World: The Divine Imagination (Disc 3, Track 8, 0:16), Sounds True (www.soundstrue.com) 2005.

4. Robert Louis Stevenson, The Silverado Squatters (1883), Travel Memoir to Napa Valley, California, 1880.

5. Holy Bible (King James Version), The Lord's Prayer, See Matt. 6:9-13.

<u>Chapter 11: The Vine and the Branches</u>
1. Holy Bible (NIV), John 15:5-17.

[5] "I am the vine; you are the branches. If you remain in me and I in you, you will bear much fruit; apart from me you can do nothing. [6] If you do not remain in me, you are like a branch that is thrown away and withers; such branches are picked up, thrown into the fire and burned. [7] If you remain in me and my words remain in you, ask whatever you wish, and it will be done for you. [8] This is to my Father's glory, that you bear much fruit, showing yourselves to be my disciples."

[9] "As the Father has loved me, so have I loved you. Now remain in my love. [10] If you keep my commands, you will remain in my love, just as I have kept my Father's commands and remain in his love. [11] I have told you this so that my joy may be in you and that your joy may be complete. [12] My command is this: Love each other as I have loved you. [13] Greater love has no one than this: to lay down one's life for one's friends. [14] You are my friends if you do what I command. [15] I no longer call you servants, because a servant does not know his master's business. Instead, I have called you friends, for everything that I learned from my Father I have made known to you. [16] You did not choose me, but I chose you and appointed you so that you might go and bear fruit—fruit that will last—and so that

whatever you ask in my name the Father will give you. [17] This is my command: Love each other."

2. Holy Bible (King James Version), Genesis 1:3.
   And God said, Let there be light: and there was light.

3. Holy Bible (King James Version), John 1:9.
   That was the true Light, which lighteth every man that cometh into the world.

Chapter 12: Round the Table
1. Holy Bible (King James Version), Matt. 26:27-29.

Afterwords: Being Known (A Reflection on Psalm 139)
1. Krista Tippett, The Inner Landscape of Beauty, Interview with John O'Donohue, 2008. (www.onbeing.org).

go and love;

love

like

wine.

about the author

William Ruel (Bill) Hudson began writing in 2010 after the abrupt loss of his older brother, at only 30 years of age.

Sweet Mellow Red is Bill's first published work.

Bill continues work as a computer programmer, where he first learned the value of establishing authentic friendships in the midst of professional surroundings, and he finds it ironic that his first writings were logical poems (programs) read by computer chips.

Commuting into Lexington and Louisville for work, Bill lives with his wife and four children in Versailles, Kentucky.

Bill developed and launched www.beingKnown.org, a blog site, for one of his good friends in the fall of 2012, and in the spring of 2013 (on the third anniversary of his brother's death) he posted his first article: *A Texas Tune.*

Bill continues to post blogs and select poetry on the new version of the Being Known website (where readers and aspiring writers are encouraged to share their personal stories).

Contact for Bill:
wrhudson.writings@gmail.com

Made in USA - Kendallville, IN
1205771_9781735032207
12.04.2020 0802